KINGFISHER HISTORY ENCYCLOPEDIA

The Modern World

1950–Present

The years since 1950 are recent history. Some of the events may have occurred during our lifetime, or we may have seen reports of them on television or the internet. These years have seen social, technological and environmental changes never witnessed before. Politicians and policy-makers, as well as historians, have identified several important trends which will continue to transform our world: advances in science and technology, environmental pollution, ever-increasing populations, changing family structures, a growing gap between the rich and poor, and an increase in global terrorism.

KINGFISHER

KINGFISHER

Kingfisher Publications Plc
New Penderel House
283–288 High Holborn
London WC1V 7HZ
www.kingfisherpub.com

First published by Kingfisher Publications Plc in 1999
This updated edition published in 2006
Reprinted in this format in 2007
2 4 6 8 10 9 7 5 3 1
1TS/0607/PROSP/(PICA)/128MA/C

A CIP catalogue record for this book is available
from the British Library

ISBN 978 0 7534 0975 6

Printed in China

PROJECT TEAM
Project Director and Art Editor Julian Holland
Editorial team Julian Holland, Norman Brooke
Designers Julian Holland, Nigel White/RWS Studio
Picture Research Anne-Marie Ehrlich, Josie Bradbury
Maps Jeffrey Farrow

FOR KINGFISHER
Managing Editor Miranda Smith
Art Director Mike Davis
DTP Co-ordinator Nicky Studdart
Artwork Research Katie Puckett
Production Manager Oonagh Phelan

CONTRIBUTORS
Teresa Chris, Neil Grant, Ken Hills, Julian Holland, Palden Jenkins,
Elizabeth Longley, Fiona Macdonald, Hazel Martell,
Mike McGuire, Theodore Rowland-Entwhistle

INTRODUCTION

O ften, fact is stranger than fiction. Your *Kingfisher History Encyclopedia* is packed full of fascinating facts and real-life stories about the people, places and events of the past that have shaped the colourful but still turbulent world that we know today. The causes and effects of the actions and events are explained in full, giving a vivid picture of how leaders, tyrants, artists and scientists who lived hundreds of years ago have left a legacy which still impinges on people's lives at the beginning of the 21st century.

Use your *Kingfisher History Encyclopedia* to discover past events and find out how people have lived their lives over the last 40,000 years – from Stone Age cave-dwellers to the Anglo-Saxons, from the Aztecs and Incas of Central America to the Manchus in China, and from the American Revolutionary War to United Nations peace-keeping.

This user-friendly encyclopedia contains many features to help you look things up easily, or simply to have fun just browsing through. The in-depth coverage of each period of history also makes the encyclopedia perfect for all your project work and homework assignments.

The clear, informative text is accompanied by key date boxes, colourful photographs and superb illustrations and maps. At-a-glance world maps at the beginning of each volume tell you quickly the major events that happened during a particular time period. These are arranged according to continent or area of the world. At the end of the volumes there are three special feature spreads which take an overall look at the arts, architecture, and science and technology of that particular period.

Whether you use your *Kingfisher History Encyclopedia* for schoolwork or just to dip into at random, it will add considerably to your understanding of the past, and will stimulate you to explore further the lives of our ancestors.

ACKNOWLEDGEMENTS

The Publisher would like to thank the following for permission to reproduce their material. Every care has been taken to trace copyright holders. However, if there have been unintentional omissions or failure to trace copyright holders, we apologise and will, if informed, endeavour to make corrections in any future edition.

Photographs (t = top; b = bottom; m = middle; l = left; r = right)
2 NASA/Science Photo Library; 3 tl Rex Features, tr Rob Francis/Robert Harding Picture Library, br Stuart Franklin/Magnum Photos, bl G.Mendel/Magnum Photos; 4 tr Popperfoto, bl Rex Features; 5 t Hulton Getty Picture Library, m Magnum Photos, br ET Archive, bl Hulton Getty Picture Library; 6 ml Novosti/Science Photo Library, bl NASA/Science Photo Library, tr NASA/Science Photo Library; 7 t NASA/Science Photo Library, b NASA/Science Photo Library; 8 tl Robert Harding, b Marc Riboud/Magnum Photos, tr Eve Arnold/Magnum Photos; 9 tl PA Photos/Panoramic, t Corbis/Eric Gaillard/ Reuters, b Paul Lowe/Magnum Photos; 10 tr OECD, b Elliot Erwitt/Magnum Photos; 11 t Abbas/Magnum Photos, mr Popperfoto/Reuters, b European Parliament/ Airdiasol; 12 tl Hulton Getty Picture Library, tr Roger-Viollet, bl Corbis; 13 t Magnum Photos, b Griffiths/Magnum Photos; 14 tl P. Jones Griffiths/Magnum Photos, tr Getty Images/AFP, ml Danny Lyon/Magnum, b Bob Adelman/Magnum Photos; 15 t Chris Steele-Perkins/Magnum Photos, m Magnum Photos, b Thomas Hoepker/Magnum Photos; 16 tl James Natchwey/Magnum Photos, tr Rex Features, b Rex Features; 17 tr F. Scianna/ Magnum Photos, bl Liba Taylor/Robert Harding Picture Library, br Robert Harding Picture Library; 18 tl Hulton Getty Picture Library, tr Popperfoto, b Marilyn Silverstone/Magnum Photos; 19 t Pinkhassov/Magnum Photos, m Pinkhassov/Magnum Photos, b S.Franklin/ Magnum Photos; 20 tl Burt Glinn/Magnum Photos, b Jones-Griffiths/Magnum Photos; 21 t Jean Gaumy/Magnum Photos, mr Stuart Franklin/Magnum, br Steve McCurry/ Magnum Photos; 22 tl Hank Morgan/University of Massachusetts at Amherst/Science Photo Library, ml Alfred Pasieka/Science Photo Library, b Brian Brake/Science Photo Library, t Tim Davis/Science Photo Library, tr Dr Jeremy Burgess/Science Photo Library; 23 t NASA/Science Photo Library, mr NASA/Science Photo Library; 24 tr Steve McCurry/ Magnum Photos, b Bruno Barbey/Magnum Photos; 25 tl G.Peress/Magnum Photos, tr Thomas Hopker/Magnum Photos, bl Russell D. Curtis/Science Photo Library, br Martin Bond/Science Photo Library; 26 tl Robert Harding Picture Library, bl Rob Francis/Robert Harding Picture Library, tr Rene Burri/Magnum Photos; 27 ml Micha Bar-Am/Magnum Photos, br Paul Lowe/Magnum Photos; 28 tl Steve McCurry/Magnum Photos, tr Paul Lowe/ Magnum Photos, b Marilyn Silverstone/Magnum Photos; 29 tr Luc Delahaye/Magnum Photos, m Steve McCurry/Magnum Photos, mr Martin Parr/Magnum Photos, b Bruno Barbey/Magnum Photos; 30 tl G.Mendel/Magnum Photos, ml G.Mendel/Magnum Photos, b Frank Spooner Pictures/Gamma, tr Gideon Mendel/Magnum Photos; 31 t Frank Spooner Pictures/Gamma, m Frank Spooner Pictures/Gamma, b Frank Spooner Pictures/Gamma

Artwork archivists Wendy Allison, Steve Robinson
Editorial and design Aimee Johnson, Sheila Clewley, Julie Ferris, Emma Wilde, Dileri Johnston, Giles Sparrow, Joanne Brown
Artists Jonathan Adams, Hemesh Alles, Marion Appleton, Sue Barclay, R. Barnett, Noel Bateman, Simon Bishop, Richard Bonson, Nick Cannan, Vanessa Card, Tony Chance, Harry Clow, Stephen Conlin, Peter Dennis, Dave Etchell, Jeff Farrow, James Field, Ian Fish, Michael Fisher, Eugene Fleury, Chris Forsey, Dewey Franklin, Terry Gabbey, Fred Gambino, John Gillatt, Matthew Gore, Jeremy Gower, Neil Gower, Ray Grinaway, Allan Hardcastle, Nick Harris, Nicholas Hewetson, Bruce Hogarth, Christian Hook, Richard Hook, Simon Huson, John James, Peter Jarvis, John Kelly, Deborah Kindred, Adrian Lascombe, Chris Lenthall, Jason Lewis, Chris Lyon, Kevin Maddison, Shirley Mallinson, Shane Marsh, David MacAllister, Angus McBride, Stefan Morris, Jackie Moore, Teresa Morris, Frank Nichols, Chris D. Orr, Sharon Pallent, R. Payne, R. Philips, Jayne Pickering, Melvyn Pickering, Malcolm Porter, Mike Posen, Mike Roffe, Chris Rothero, David Salarya, Mike Saunders, Rodney Shackell, Rob Shone, Mark Stacey, Paul Stangroom, Branca Surla, Smiljka Surla, Stephen Sweet, Mike Taylor, George Thompson, Martin Wilson, David Wright, Paul Wright

CONTENTS

THE WORLD AT A GLANCE 1950–present

This period was dominated by the Cold War between communist nations and the capitalist West. The United States and the USSR played leading parts. These two were also involved in the space race. The USSR was the first to send a man into space, and the USA the first to put a man on the Moon. Changes in the USSR led to the end of the Cold War but created uncertainty about the future as nationalists demanded independence.

In western Europe, the European Union encouraged economic growth and worked towards political union. In Africa, many nations became independent, but faced severe economic problems as well as droughts and famines. In southeast Asia, technology and industry developed, and Japanese business became the most successful in the world. China experienced a cultural revolution and Indochina was devastated by a whole series of wars.

NORTH AMERICA

The second half of the 20th century was the high point of development of the USA, which led the way materially and culturally. By now, the US west coast was as much a centre for the film and aircraft industries as the east coast, and home to many futuristic ideas. The USA led the way in the nuclear arms race and was equal to the USSR in the space race. The 1950s saw growing prosperity, though this led to troubles in the 1960s over civil rights and social issues. American culture reached its high point in music, films, inventions and new ideas in the 1970s, though rocked by war in Vietnam and the exposure of government corruption. Since the 1980s, computer technology and free-market economics brought economic boom, the space shuttle and the end of the Cold War. The USA acted as a global policeman in a complex world. Its international policy caused resentment among some groups, and the USA increasingly became a target of terrorists. In 2001, an Islamic fundamentalist terrorist group called Al-Qaeda hijacked planes and crashed them in New York and Washington, DC.

NORTH AMERICA

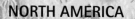

CENTRAL AND SOUTH AMERICA

CENTRAL AND SOUTH AMERICA

Until the 1970s, there was a battle between right-wing dictators and left-wing revolutionaries in Latin America. Poverty, power and guerrilla wars were the big issues. As the continent grew richer and more liberal governments came to power, these pressures eased. The Catholic Church also lost ground, and rainforest destruction, government corruption, human rights and the drugs trade grew as new issues. Civil wars in countries like Peru and Nicaragua were resolved, and in the 1990s Latin America, now industrialized, played an increasing role in global affairs.

EUROPE

Ruined by World War II and overshadowed by the Cold War, Europe made a dramatic recovery in the 1950s–1970s, beginning a long process of co-operation through the founding of the European Union. Europe worked with a 'social market' model of economics, with ample welfare and social systems which, by the 1990s, became a burden. Despite crises, such as the Hungarian uprising of 1956 and the 'Prague Spring' of 1968, Europe remained in peace. The greatest breakthrough was the ending of the Cold War, which reunited Germany and brought reconciliation between east and west, though ugly scenes such as the Yugoslavian civil wars of the 1990s hindered progress. Environmental and social concerns were important, especially after the Russian nuclear disaster at Chernobyl in 1986. The European Union became the dominant economic and political organization in the region, expanding its membership and launching a common currency.

ASIA

During this period, the fortunes of Asia rose again. The Maoist era in China brought mixed results, some impressive, some disastrous. They led to reforms in the 1980s and to China's re-entry into the world's market economy. Japan became the economic and technological powerhouse of Asia, and fuelled great economic growth in southeast Asia from the early 1970s. India modernized in the 1970s, though conflicts continued with Pakistan. The withdrawal of colonial powers, the Vietnam War, the rise of Islamic and Confucian values, the fall of the USSR in Central Asia and the globalization of the world economy have all had a great effect on Asia.

EUROPE

ASIA

MIDDLE EAST

AFRICA

AUSTRALASIA

Australia and New Zealand became leading countries, although they had to acclimatize to an increase in contact with Asia. Australia became one of the world's wealthiest countries. Polynesia became a tourist destination, but also a place for atomic bomb testing.

AUSTRALASIA

AFRICA

After a promising start in the 1960s, when most states gained independence, Africa was troubled with wars, corruption, famine, social crises and the AIDS virus. Foreign interference and over-exploitation were common. In South Africa, torn by apartheid, reform came in 1990 and brought the dawn of a new multi-racial society. Zimbabwe and other countries are still in political and economic turmoil.

MIDDLE EAST

Oil-rich, the Middle East witnessed great extremes of wealth and suffering during this period. Rising Islamic fundamentalism had mixed outcomes, disturbing peace, yet helping the poor and downtrodden. Caught between different world powers, war and interference by foreign powers were common.

THE COLD WAR 1945–1989

After the end of World War II, tensions between East and West and the build-up of nuclear weapons almost brought the world to the brink of a third world war.

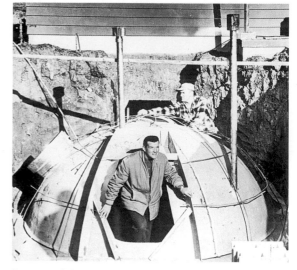

A 1962 cartoon, produced at the time of the Cuba missile crisis, shows the two superpower leaders arm-wrestling for power. The USSR's Nikita Khrushchev (1894–1971), on the left, faces the US president John F. Kennedy (1917–63). They are both sitting on their own nuclear weapons.

The USSR and the USA fought together as allies against Germany and Japan in World War II, but in 1945, these two great countries, known as superpowers, became rivals and then enemies. This division became known as the Cold War, a war conducted in the main without fighting. The USA and USSR 'fought' by making threats and by strengthening their armed forces.

Both countries built up an enormous stockpile of nuclear weapons. Peaceful, friendly contacts between their peoples ceased. The USSR became completely shut off from the rest of the world by Soviet troops. The British statesman Sir Winston Churchill memorably described the frontier between East and West as an 'iron curtain' in a speech that he gave in Missouri, USA, on March 5, 1946.

The Cold War dominated world politics for many years. On one side, the United States became the leader of NATO, a military alliance of Western nations ranged against the communist powers. On the other side, the USSR dominated the Warsaw Pact, a military alliance of East European states that backed communism.

Because of the serious threat of nuclear war between East and West during the 1960s, many Americans built fall-out shelters in their back gardens.

BERLIN: THE DIVIDED CITY

In 1945, the USA, France and Britain took control of West Germany and the USSR controlled East Germany. The capital, Berlin, inside East Germany, was also divided, and in 1948, the Soviets closed all access to west Berlin. The Western powers brought in essential supplies by air until the Russians lifted the blockade in May 1949. From 1949 to 1958, three million people escaped from east to west Berlin. In 1961, East Germany closed off this escape route by building the Berlin Wall through the centre of the city. It crossed tramlines and roads, and created an area on either side known as no man's land.

▲ The Berlin Wall, built in 1961 to divide east and west Berlin, finally fell in November 1989.

▶ By 1949, most European states had joined rival alliances. Warsaw pact countries supported the USSR. Members of NATO backed the USA.

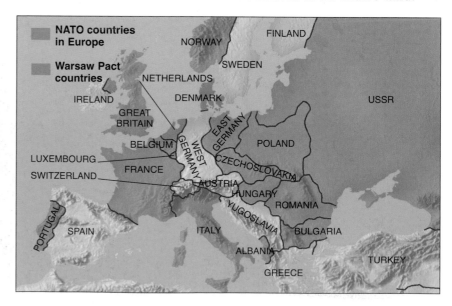

NATO countries in Europe

Warsaw Pact countries

FINLAND
NORWAY
SWEDEN
NETHERLANDS
IRELAND
DENMARK
USSR
GREAT BRITAIN
EAST GERMANY
BELGIUM
WEST GERMANY
POLAND
LUXEMBOURG
CZECHOSLOVAKIA
SWITZERLAND
FRANCE
AUSTRIA
HUNGARY
ROMANIA
YUGOSLAVIA
PORTUGAL
SPAIN
ITALY
BULGARIA
ALBANIA
TURKEY
GREECE

CUBAN MISSILE CRISIS

Although the USA and the USSR never actually fought, they came close to it. The world held its breath for a whole week in October 1962 when the US president, John F. Kennedy, received air force photographs showing that the USSR was building missile launch sites in Cuba. From there, the nuclear missiles could reach and destroy many US cities. On October 22, the president ordered a naval blockade of Cuba. The United States made plans to invade Cuba, and the world braced itself for nuclear war. Finally, on October 28, Nikita Khrushchev, the Soviet leader, backed down and agreed to remove the missiles and destroy the Cuban launch sites. The crisis was over.

THE END OF THE COLD WAR

In the 1980s, the friendly relationship between US president Ronald Reagan and the Soviet leader Mikhail Gorbachev helped to reduce Cold War tensions, and by 1987, they had agreed to abolish medium-range nuclear missiles. In 1989, Gorbachev allowed the communist countries of eastern Europe to elect democratic governments, and in 1991, the USSR broke up into 15 republics. The Cold War was over. On March 12, 1999, Hungary, Poland and the Czech Republic joined NATO. The joining ceremony was held at the Harry S. Truman memorial library in Independence, Missouri, in the United States.

◀ Francis Gary Powers was the pilot of an American U–2 spy plane which was shot down over Soviet territory in 1960. He was released in exchange for the imprisoned Soviet spymaster Rudolf Abel.

▼ Czech students tried to stop Soviet tanks in Prague, in August 1968. The USSR feared that independent actions by Warsaw Pact members might weaken its power, so the Russians moved into Czechoslovakia.

▶ During the Cold War, many groups of people, such as the Peace Pledge Union, were formed to try and influence governments and stop the spread of nuclear weapons.

◀ Supporters of the Campaign for Nuclear Disarmament (CND) marched through London in 1983 to demonstrate against the deployment of Cruise and Trident nuclear missiles on British soil.

IN SPACE 1957–present

Space exploration began in 1957 when the USSR launched *Sputnik I.* In 2001, the first space tourist paid for a return flight to space.

The development of technology during World War II helped scientists to realize that one day it might be possible for people to travel in space. Cold War rivalry between the USA and the USSR triggered a space race. Both sides felt that being the first nation in space would increase their prestige. They also hoped that space science would help them develop new, more powerful weapons.

The Soviets achieved the first 'space first' when they sent a satellite into orbit around the Earth in 1957. Soon, both sides were investing enormous amounts of time and money in space science. The Soviets achieved another space first in 1961 when Yuri Gagarin became the first man in space. Other notable achievements by both countries included probes being sent to the Moon and past Venus, further manned flights, spacewalks and the launch of communications satellites.

The *Apollo* programme of space flights enabled the USA to land men on the Moon. Between July 1969 and December 1972, the USA successfully carried out six of these missions, the last three involving the use of a Lunar Roving Vehicle.

Sputnik 1 was launched by Russia on October 4, 1957. The satellite was used to broadcast scientific data and orbited the Earth for six months.

Russian cosmonaut Yuri Gagarin in the cabin of *Vostok 1*, the spacecraft in which he became the first person to orbit the Earth on April 12, 1961.

MAN ON THE MOON

In 1961, the United States president, John F. Kennedy, said that his scientists would send a man to the Moon by 1970. In fact, the first manned Moon landing took place on July 20, 1969 with the American *Apollo 11* mission. The crew consisted of Neil Armstrong, the first man to set foot on the Moon, Edwin 'Buzz' Aldrin, who was the second man to walk on the Moon, and Michael Collins who remained in lunar orbit in the command and service module. Armstrong described walking on the Moon as 'one small step for man, one giant leap for mankind'.

In the run-up to the *Apollo* flights, the American Gemini programme was designed to teach astronauts how to cope with space travel. In November 1966 'Buzz' Aldrin carried out three spacewalks high over the Earth.

The end of the Cold War led the two superpowers to scale down their space programmes. However, in 1993 they agreed to work together to develop a multinational space station – the International Space Station – the first parts of which were launched into orbit in late 1998. The International Space Station received its first resident crew in 2000.

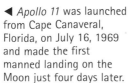

◄ *Apollo 11* was launched from Cape Canaveral, Florida, on July 16, 1969 and made the first manned landing on the Moon just four days later.

SPACE SHUTTLES

In the USA, the National Aeronautics & Space Administration (NASA) developed a reusable space vehicle, the space shuttle, which could take off like a rocket and return to Earth like a plane. The launch of the first shuttle in 1981 marked a new phase in space exploration. Since then, space shuttles have carried people and cargo to and from orbiting spacecraft and space stations. In 2003, the US shuttle fleet was grounded after the shuttle *Columbia* exploded on its return to Earth. But it was relaunched again in 2005 with the shuttle *Discovery*, which docked to the International Space Station.

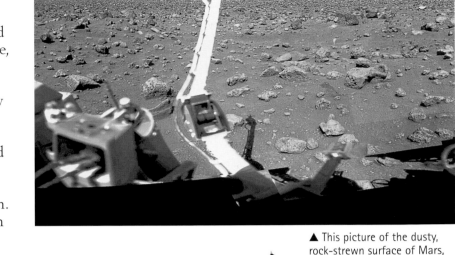

▲ This picture of the dusty, rock-strewn surface of Mars, was taken by one of the two US *Viking* landers in 1975. Part of the spacecraft is visible in the foreground.

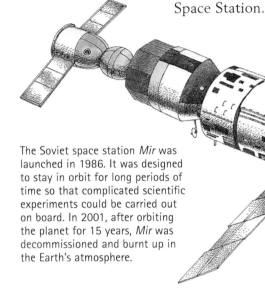

The Soviet space station *Mir* was launched in 1986. It was designed to stay in orbit for long periods of time so that complicated scientific experiments could be carried out on board. In 2001, after orbiting the planet for 15 years, *Mir* was decommissioned and burnt up in the Earth's atmosphere.

EXPLORING DEEP SPACE

Unmanned space probes have flown by, or landed on, every planet in the Solar System except Pluto. Soviet probes landed on Venus in 1975 and sent back pictures. In 1977, the US launched the two *Voyager* missions which travelled around the Solar System using the 'slingshot' technique – the spacecraft being flung from planet to planet by their gravitational fields. Before they disappeared into deep space, they transmitted valuable data and photographs of Jupiter, Saturn, Uranus and Neptune.

The Hubble space telescope, launched by the US in 1990, enabled scientists to produce images of objects billions of light years way, and provided information about the Universe. In 2004, the US rovers *Spirit* and *Opportunity* landed on Mars and sent pictures of the red planet to Earth. They also studied the soil and rocks on Mars.

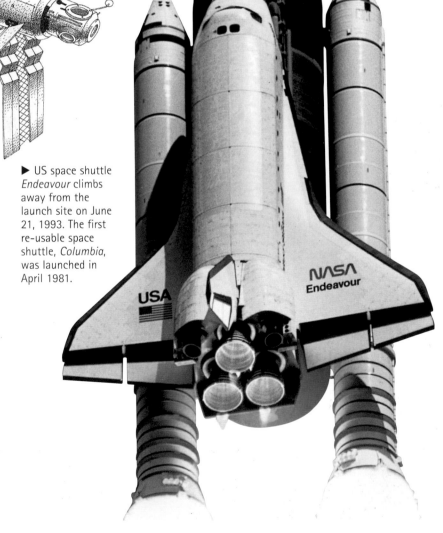

► US space shuttle *Endeavour* climbs away from the launch site on June 21, 1993. The first re-usable space shuttle, *Columbia*, was launched in April 1981.

CHINA 1949–present

In 1949, Mao Zedong and the communist party came to power and transformed this battle-weary country. Today, the Chinese economy is one of the largest in the world.

By the 1990s, China was far removed from its previous peasant economy. All types of sophisticated electronic equipment were now being manufactured and exported abroad.

▼ Mao Zedong tried to solve the problem of food shortages in China by creating collective farms. Here, rice farmers are at work in the southern region of Guangxi in the early 1960s.

The communist party came to power in China in 1949, and Mao Zedong, their leader, became chairman of the Peoples' Republic of China. Civil war, and the war with Japan, had left the land poor and many people were starving. Roads, railways, schools and hospitals could not meet the peoples' needs. Many in the new government believed that they should follow the example of the communists in Russia. Mao did not agree with the move to industrialization, because he believed in a peasant economy. Land was redistributed to the peasants, but Mao resigned in 1959.

While the government followed the Russian example, Mao started his own 'Cultural Revolution' in 1966, aimed at wiping out feudalism and capitalism. In 1970, he was made supreme commander.

Mao transformed Chinese society. Collective farms grew basic foods and industry produced more iron and steel.

To control the population, the Chinese government encouraged couples to have only one child.

'Barefoot doctors' provided medical care to people in the countryside and children learned to read and write. Mao wrote and distributed widely 'The Thoughts of Chairman Mao'. It was required reading and everyone carried a copy with them wherever they went. Even the simplest peasants were able to quote from it.

▲ The centrepiece of the 2008 Olympics is the Beijing National Stadium, designed to look like a bird's nest. The arena will seat 80,000 peple.

► The elaborate closing ceremony of the 2004 Athens Olympics featured a colourful dance routine by Chinese children to show that the Games were heading for Beijing in four years' time.

THE 2008 OLYMPIC GAMES

The historic Chinese capital, Beijing, was chosen to host the 2008 summer Olympic Games by the International Olympic Committee in July 2001. During the lengthy selection process, the Chinese bid beat off strong competition from Toronto (Canada), Paris (France), Istanbul (Turkey) and Osaka (Japan). The Beijing games promise to be the biggest in the history of the Olympics, with around 10,500 athletes taking part in 302 events covering more than 30 sports – from boxing and archery to wrestling and water polo. Not all the events will take place in the Chinese capital. Football matches will be held in the cities of Tianjin, Shanghai, Shenyang and Qinhuangdo, while the sailing events will be hosted by the port of Qingdao and the equestrian competition will take place in Hong Kong. A number of events will make their Olympic debut at the 2008 games, including BMX biking and marathon swimming races over a distance of 10km.

ECONOMIC GROWTH

China's economy almost came to a grinding halt during the Cultural Revolution. After Mao's death in 1976, the Chinese government under its new leader, Deng Xiaoping, began to reform the economy by opening up to the rest of the world and encouraging foreign trade and investment. The economy grew so fast that by 2005, the Gross Domestic Product was ten times higher than it had been in 1978 and the economy had become the second-largest in the world after the USA.

BUILDING BOOM

China's cities have experienced a building boom in recent years as stunning high-rise buildings have transformed the skylines of Shanghai and other major urban centres. The country's biggest construction project since the Great Wall has been the Three Gorges dam, built across the Yangtze River. The largest hydroelectric river dam in the world, it is expected to meet more than one-tenth of China's electricity needs when it becomes fully operational in 2009.

POPULATION GROWTH

China saw a massive increase in its population, which had reached more than 1.2 billion by 1990. In an effort to control this fast growth, the Chinese government rewarded one-child families with priority housing and medical care. The figure is expected to reach a peak of 1.5 billion by the year 2050.

▼ A magnificent fireworks display marked the return of Hong Kong to Chinese ownership on June 30, 1997 when Britain's 99-year lease on the territory officially came to an end.

WORLD ECONOMY 1950 – present

The industrialized countries of the world had improved their standard of living since 1950, but many poorer countries saw little or no improvement.

The flag of the European Union, the successor to the European Economic Community. The EU is made up of 27 member states from across Europe.

▼ There was panic trading on the floor of the New York Stock Exchange in October 1987. In that year, stockmarkets around the world suffered a dramatic downward revaluation in the value of shares.

After the end of World War II, the USA and many countries in western Europe enjoyed a rapid growth in their economies. After the war, there was an enormous amount of re-building to be done, particularly in Europe. There was full employment and the amount people were paid, compared to what things cost to buy, steadily climbed. This rise in 'standard of living' also applied to a slightly lesser extent to countries such as Australia and New Zealand, as well as southeast Asian states such as Hong Kong, Singapore and Taiwan.

This prosperity came to a sudden halt in 1973 when the price of crude oil started to increase. The Organization of Petroleum Exporting Countries (OPEC) was founded in 1960 to get the best price on world markets for its member states' oil. OPEC members include many Middle Eastern Arab states as well as Venezuela, Algeria, Indonesia, Nigeria and the Gabon. Between 1973 and 1974, OPEC

The OECD (Organization for Economic Co-operation and Development) was created to protect weak nations from powerful market forces and aid economic development.

quadrupled the price of oil, and this led to a worldwide energy crisis. Poorer nations were badly hit by the rise in oil prices. By 1981, this had increased almost twenty times and their economies had to be supported by loans from the West. In the advanced nations, the energy crisis caused inflation, because the rise in oil prices was passed on in the form of raised prices for goods, and unemployment everywhere rose as less goods were exported.

COMMON MARKETS

Throughout the world, neighbouring states, or states with shared economic interests, have joined together to form powerful international associations. Some groups of states have also set up economic communities known as 'common markets'. Within these markets, members buy and sell at favourable rates. They agree to protect one another from economic competition from the outside.

In Asia, there are the Asia-Pacific Economic Co-operation Group (APEC) and the Association of Southeast Asian Nations (ASEAN). The North American Free Trade Agreement (NAFTA), originally the US and Canada, now includes Mexico. The Group of Eight, or G-8, is a group of major countries that meets to monitor the world economic situation. The European Union (EU) is the successor of the European Economic Community (EEC) of the 1950s. It is made up of 27 members from across Europe and forms a significant world trading-block. Many of the EU members share a single currency – the euro.

The collapse of the Soviet Union in the early 1990s meant that the former communist countries had to compete with other third world countries. While the richer Western nations provided aid to poorer countries in the past, they remained reluctant to share a substantial part of their wealth or expertise.

By 2004, it was estimated that the world's oil reserves amounted to around 1,293 billion barrels, of which over 700 billion barrels were to be found in the Middle East.

▲ In January 2002, 12 members of the European Union stopped using their own individual currencies and adopted a common currency called the euro.

Policy decisions of the European Union are made by the European Parliament. It is split between Brussels, Luxemborg and Strasbourg (above). The parliament is made up of more than 730 representatives, directly elected by their member countries. Current members include France, Germany, the Netherlands, Belguim, Luxemborg, the United Kingdom, Ireland, Greece, Spain, Denmark, Portugal and Austria.

WARS IN ASIA 1950 – present

Japan's defeat and the collapse of colonial rule led to fighting between political rivals throughout Asia. The superpowers took sides and began to join in.

In 1945, French colonial rule was restored to Vietnam. French Foreign Legion troops were sent to North Vietnam in 1953 to try to suppress a communist uprising.

In 1950, many countries in the East had still not recovered from Japanese invasions during World War II. People needed peace and stability, but many nations were at war. These wars caused further damage to people, cities and the land. Eastern countries no longer wished to be colonies of distant European powers. And the old colonial masters (France, Britain and the Netherlands) wanted to hold on to these potentially rich lands.

Fighting broke out in Vietnam and its neighbours Laos, Thailand and Cambodia, as well as in Indonesia, Malaysia, Burma and the Philippines. These wars were often complicated by political differences between rival groups seeking independence. The situation became more dangerous still when the Soviet, Chinese and American superpowers joined in with offers of money, weapons or technical advice for one side or the other.

Australian soldiers were part of the United Nations forces that by the end of 1950 had pushed the North Koreans back as far as the border with China.

▼ Fighting between rival political groups flared up in many parts of Asia between 1946 and 1988 following Japan's defeat in World War II and the collapse of European colonial power.

THE KOREAN WAR

The Korean War began when communist North Korea attacked South Korea in June 1950. The United Nations quickly authorized its members to aid South Korea. The United States, together with 16 other countries, began sending in troops. Within two months, North Korean troops had captured most of South Korea. In September 1950, UN forces mounted a massive land, sea and air assault at Inchon, near Seoul. The UN troops recaptured most of South Korea and advanced into the North. By November, they had reached the North Korean border with China. Chinese troops then entered the fighting and forced the UN forces to retreat south. A ceasefire ended the war in July 1953.

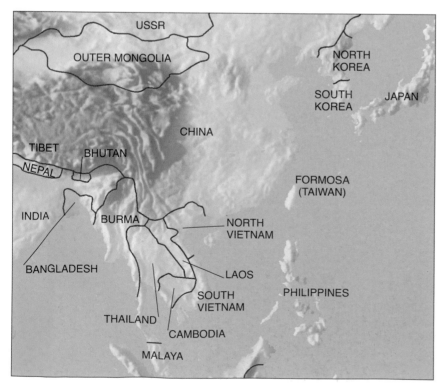

▲ Between 1948 and 1960, British troops were sent to Malaya to fight the communist guerrilla offensive. Here, soldiers of a jungle patrol rest under a temporary shelter.

During the Vietnam War (1964–75), many parts of the country were devastated. Thousands of civilians were killed, and others were made homeless and fled as refugees to neighbouring countries. Peace finally came in 1976 when Vietnam was united.

Ho-Chi Minh (1892–1969) was a founder member of the French Communist Party and a revolutionary Vietnamese leader. He led the struggle against the French colonial rule of Vietnam and American-supported South Vietnam.

WAR IN VIETNAM

After the French were defeated by Vietnamese communists in 1954, the country was temporarily divided into two – north and south. Planned elections for the country did not take place and the communists in the north started giving aid to South Vietnamese communists, the Viet Cong, to help them overthrow the government of Ngo Dinh Diem.

In 1965, the United States sent the first troops to help the south and by 1969 there were more than half a million US troops in Vietnam. After Richard Nixon became US president in 1969, he began to withdraw troops. A ceasefire was signed in 1973, and the remainder of American soldiers went home. During the war, more than 57,000 Americans were killed or went missing in action.

CIVIL WAR IN CAMBODIA

In Cambodia, a guerrilla army, the Khmer Rouge, was led by Pol Pot, and they sought to overthrow the government of Lon Nol. The Khmer Rouge took over Cambodia in 1975 and Pol Pot became prime minister. His terror regime ended in 1979 when he was overthrown by Vietnamese troops.

▲ After Richard Nixon (1913–94) became president in 1969, he began to withdraw US troops from Vietnam. In 1973, a ceasefire was signed and the US troops were withdrawn.

◄ In Cambodia, Pol Pot (1926–98) was the leader of the Khmer Rouge guerrillas. They fought a long civil war beginning in 1963, and finally took over the country in 1975. Over the following three years, it is estimated that between two and four million people were executed or died of famine and disease.

KEY DATES

1950	North Korean forces invade South Korea
1953	Ceasefire in Korea
1954	Vietminh communists defeat the French and Vietnam is divided
1963	Civil war starts in Cambodia
1965	First US troops land in Vietnam
1969	Richard Nixon becomes US president
1973	All US troops withdrawn from Vietnam
1975	Pol Pot takes over Cambodia
1979	Pol Pot deposed by Vietnamese forces
1993	First free elections in Cambodia for 20 years

CIVIL RIGHTS 1950–present

Civil rights are the basic freedoms and rights of people living within a community. The rights are guaranteed by laws and customs that give everyone fair treatment.

Re-formed during the 1950s, the Ku Klux Klan harassed blacks and minority groups in the USA. They burned crosses to intimidate people.

The idea of civil rights in the West dates back to the writings of many Ancient Greek and Roman philosophers and to the ideas of Judaism and Christianity. In some countries, civil rights are protected by a written constitution. In the USA and in other democratic countries, such as the United Kingdom, they consist of laws and customs built up over hundreds of years.

Civil rights mean that people must be treated fairly and equally, no matter what their sex, religion or ethnic origin. They should be given the freedom to express what they believe in speech or in the media. They should also have the right to organize a political party, to have a fair trial and to vote in elections. Many oppressive regimes still ignore civil rights and abuse their power.

A woman holds up posters of relatives who went missing in Argentina in the 1970s. She is a member of the 'Mothers of the Plaza de Mayo', a group of civil rights activists.

Many rights have been won only after a long and painful struggle. During the 1950s and 1960s, Dr Martin Luther King led the civil rights campaign in the USA to win equality for black Americans.

In the early 1960s, many southern US states operated a colour bar. This taxi was only for the use of coloured people. Other forms of public transport were similarly segregated.

MARTIN LUTHER KING

The Reverend Martin Luther King Jr (1929–68) was a Baptist minister and the leader of the US civil rights movement of the 1950s and 1960s. On August 28, 1963, he led a march on Washington DC where he gave a famous speech that began, 'I have a dream...' His dream was of a future in which his country would live by the ideals of freedom and liberty on which it had been founded. On April 4, 1968, he was shot dead by James Earl Ray. From 1983, the third Monday in January has been designated a federal holiday in his honour.

CIVIL RIGHTS ABUSES

In South Africa, Nelson Mandela was sent to prison in 1962 for opposing apartheid (the separation of whites and non-whites). Many governments and people from all over the world campaigned to end apartheid by holding demonstrations, boycotting goods from South Africa and stopping all sporting links. F. W. de Klerk became president in 1989 and he began to dismantle apartheid. Mandela was released in 1990, the year apartheid was abolished. In 1994, he was elected South Africa's first black president.

In 1976, Argentina was taken over by a military junta. They suppressed opposition by arresting thousands of people and holding them in prison without trial. Between 20,000 and 30,000 people were never seen again and they became known by their families as '*los desaparecidos*', the 'disappeared ones'. Similar brutality was used by the military regime led by General Pinochet in Chile between 1973 and 1990.

PROTECTING CIVIL RIGHTS

International bodies, such as the United Nations and the European Court of Human Rights, protect civil rights. Other organizations, such as Amnesty International, campaign on behalf of people who are persecuted. However, some governments continue to obstruct civil rights. Dictators and single-party states deny rights to ordinary people because they see them as a threat.

▲ In the 1970s and 1980s, Chile was ruled by a military junta. Ordinary citizens were arrested and many were never seen again. The Catholic Church denounced the violence against innocent people. They held religious services for detained or missing people.

◀ In the South African city of Johannesburg in the 1980s, many black and coloured people were moved into slums and shanty towns to make more room for the homes of white people.

When European settlers first arrived in Australia in the 18th and 19th centuries, the Aborigines, the original inhabitants of the land, were driven off their traditional hunting grounds. Many also died from European diseases brought in by the settlers. The Australian government still does not recognize that the Aborigines were the original custodians of the land before European settlers arrived in 1788.

15

TERRORISM 1952–present

During the last 50 years, many people used violence to promote particular political causes, often aimed at overthrowing the established order.

During 1981, some members of the Irish Republican Army (IRA) who were serving prison sentences in Northern Ireland for terrorist offences went on hunger strike. When one of them died, there was rioting.

▼ In 1988, an American jumbo jet was blown up by a bomb in mid-air over the Scottish town of Lockerbie, killing 270 people. Libyan terrorists were suspected of being responsible for this act.

S ome groups of people use violence (terrorism) to gain publicity and win support for a political cause. They are often called freedom fighters by their supporters. Terrorists murder and kidnap people, set off bombs and hijack aircraft. The reasons behind terrorism are not always the same. Some people want to spread their own political beliefs while others (nationalists or liberationists) want to establish a separate state for peoples who do not have a country of their own. For example, in the Middle East, terrorists have kidnapped people and carried out bombing campaigns to draw attention to the cause of the Palestinian people who do not have a homeland.

In Spain, an extreme group, *Euzkada Ta Askatasuna* (ETA) began a terrorist campaign in the 1960s to pressurize the government into creating a separate state for the Basque people. Similarly, in Northern Ireland, Nationalist groups such as the Irish Republican Army (IRA) escalated their terrorist campaign in the 1970s against British rule in the province.

In April 1995, a bomb exploded and destroyed the Federal Office building in Oklahoma City, USA. It was planted by an American citizen opposed to federal taxes and laws.

In 2001, an Islamic fundamentalist terrorist group, called Al-Qaeda, launched devastating terrorist attacks on the United States of America. In 2002 and 2003 there were further attacks by the same group in Bali, Saudi Arabia and Morocco. In 2004, there were triple the amount of serious international terrorist incidents, with 651 attacks reported. In July 2005, Al-Qaeda was responsible for a series of coordinated suicide bomb attacks on the London transport system. Britain and many other countries joined the USA in launching a 'war on terror'.

FAMINE IN AFRICA 1967-present

Africa has suffered periodic drought and famine since ancient times. More recently, civil war in newly independent states has only added to the misery.

In 1985, the pop musician Bob Geldof organized the Live Aid music concerts. These raised £50 million to help the victims of the famine in Ethiopia.

Widespread famines have occurred periodically in most parts of sub-Saharan Africa since ancient times. Factors such as a failure of the annual rains, poor soil conditions and negligible food reserves have all played a part in these tragedies. Following independence, in the latter half of the 20th century, civil wars have added to the misery.

CIVIL UNREST AND FAMINE

Most of the worst famines during this period happened in countries that suffered civil unrest. In Nigeria, the people who lived in the east of the country were the Christian Ibo tribe. They were oppressed by the majority Islamic Hausa and Fulani peoples. When tens of thousands of Ibos were massacred, the Eastern Region declared its independence as the state of Biafra in May 1967. War continued between the two sides until January 1970. It is believed that more than a million Biafrans died because the Nigerians stopped emergency food getting through.

Civil strife in Mozambique in the 1980s led to the almost total collapse of health care, education and food production. By the beginning of the 1990s, nearly a million people had died and another million and a half had fled and were refugees in neighbouring countries.

During the 1991–93 civil war in Somalia, it is thought that about 300,000 people starved to death because the war made it too dangerous to deliver food aid.

▼ Zaire has had periods of military uprising and civil strife which has made life dangerous for foreign aid workers. In 1994, the arrival of hundreds of thousands of refugees from neighbouring Rwanda prompted massive aid from international relief agencies.

Ethiopia suffered from drought and famine for many years. Between 1977 and 1991, the combination of civil war and famine killed millions of Ethiopians.

In Ethiopia, the combination of the withdrawal of aid from the USSR, drought and a civil war in the 1970s and 1980s led to millions of people dying from famine. Through the Western media, people all round the world became aware of the catastrophe. International relief charities, such as the Red Cross and Oxfam, the Live Aid pop concerts of 1985 and various governments all provided vast amounts of aid for the victims.

▲ Foreign aid is not only used to provide food for the starving people of Africa. This project provided clean water for a community in Kenya. Projects like this help to improve the health of the local people.

17

NEW NATIONS 1950–present

Following centuries of rule by colonial powers, many nations have gained their independence – achieved through war, terrorism or more peaceful means.

Independence was granted to Ghana (formerly the Gold Coast) by Britain in 1957. The Duchess of Kent represented the British queen at the ceremony in the capital, Accra. In the following years, the country suffered from government corruption and military coups.

After World War II, the leaders of many European-ruled colonial countries felt the growing pressure from their people for independence from their foreign 'masters'. The days of colonial rule were rapidly coming to an end. During the 1950s and 1960s, many peoples in Africa and southeast Asia fought for their independence. Their people believed that they had a right to own and control their own countries. Many of these independence movements were led by men and women of courage and vision. They were frequently imprisoned, but in some cases eventually gained power.

Many of these countries used military force to win independence from colonial rule. European nations would not give up their power and so groups like the Mau Mau in Kenya launched terrorist campaigns. In some states, for example Egypt in 1952–53, independence was achieved only after the army took control.

The British gained control of Malaya in 1786. In September 1963, Malaya, Singapore, Sarawak and Sabah joined together to create the independent Federation of Malaysia. Singapore left the organization two years later.

RANDOM BORDERS

In Africa, numerous civil wars sprung up as the European powers gradually withdrew. One of the most common reason for this was that, where the land had been previously divided up between the European settlers, little attention was paid to the existing tribal boundaries. When the Europeans left, several tribes were often left to dispute the ownership and control of that country. When this happened in Nigeria, with the declaration of an independent Biafran state in 1967, millions of people died of starvation.

Britain granted full independence to Nigeria in 1960. Since then the country, one of the largest in Africa and a major oil producer, has suffered from a major civil war, economic problems and the restrictions of military rule.

STRUGGLE FOR SURVIVAL

Today, nearly all the former colonies are independent. Some maintain ties, as do members of the British Commonwealth. Others, such as the Organization for African Unity (OAU), have formed new alliances. Many former colonies are still economically dependent. World trade is controlled by Europe, the USA and Japan, as well as by multinational companies. It is hard for new nations not to fall into debt when they do not have financial control.

EASTERN EUROPE

The end of the Cold War and the collapse of the USSR at the end of the 1980s led to the countries around Russia's borders gaining their freedom from Soviet rule. In Czechoslovakia, free elections were held in 1990 for the first time since 1946. At the beginning of 1993, Czechoslovakia ceased to exist and was replaced by the states of the Czech Republic and Slovakia.

Between 1991 and 1992, Yugoslavia became divided as the states of Slovenia, Bosnia-Herzegovina, Macedonia and Croatia declared independence. Thousands of people were killed in the civil wars that followed. In 2003, Serbia and Montenegro replaced Yugoslavia on the map. In 2006, they broke apart to become independent nations.

Turkmenistan, on the eastern coast of the Caspian Sea, became a republic of the USSR in 1925. Following the break-up of the Soviet Union in 1991, this mainly Muslim country declared independence and joined the Commonwealth of Independent States (CIS), consisting of 12 of the 15 former Soviet republics.

▲ After the break-up of the USSR in 1991, the Muslim state of Uzbekistan became independent and joined the Commonwealth of Independent States (CIS). Food shortages in 1992 led to civil unrest and riots in the capital, Tashkent.

◀ Bosnia and Herzegovina became part of what was to be known as Yugoslavia at the end of World War I. Nationalist feeling grew after the death of President Tito in 1980. Independence was declared in 1992 against the wishes of the Serbian population and a bitter civil war broke out. Thousands of people lost their lives, while others lost their homes and became refugees.

WARS IN THE MIDDLE EAST 1956 – present

Following the formation of the state of Israel in 1948 there have been many tensions in the Middle East that have led to bitter disputes and even war.

The lands around Jerusalem have been believed for centuries by Jews to be the traditional home of the Jewish people. After World War II, many Jewish refugees settled in Palestine although the area was occupied by Arab peoples. The state of Israel was formed in 1948 and fighting broke out with neighbouring Arab countries and continued on and off for many years.

In 1956, Egypt took over the control of the Suez Canal which was owned by Britain and France. Because it felt threatened, Israel invaded Egyptian territory in Sinai, and Britain and France attacked the canal area. There was international disapproval, and the USA and the USSR both called for a ceasefire. UN troops moved in to keep the peace after the withdrawal of Israeli, British and French troops.

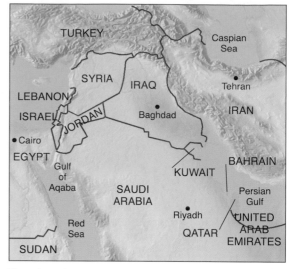

There have been many conflicts in the Middle East between Israeli, Palestinian and Arab peoples, particularly since 1948. Some areas of territory are still in dispute.

Tensions continued to grow in the 1960s between Israel and the Arab countries of Egypt, Jordan and Syria. They were aided by several other Arab countries including Iraq, Kuwait, Saudi Arabia, Algeria and Sudan. Both sides were hostile and unwilling to negotiate differences. Both sides were also occupied with preparing their troops for a possible armed conflict. In May 1967, Egypt closed the Gulf of Aqaba to Israeli shipping.

The Six Day War took place June 5–10, 1967. In a surprise attack, Israeli bombers destroyed Egyptian planes, and then sent in troops to capture the Egyptian soldiers left in Sinai.

▼ The Yom Kippur War began in 1973 when Egypt and Syria launched a surprise attack on Israel after it refused to give up land captured during the Six Day War.

In 1980, Iraq invaded Iran. The two countries fought a long and bitter war which was not to end until August 1988 and which cost the lives of over a million of their soldiers, with nearly two million wounded.

Saddam Hussein (1937–2006) was the leader of Iraq from 1979 to 2003. He fought a costly war against Iran (1980–88) and invaded Kuwait in August 1990. In 2003, a US-led military campaign overthrew him. He was executed in 2006.

THE SIX DAY WAR

In June 1967, the Israeli air-force launched a surprise air attack on the Arab forces' air bases which put them completely out of action. Over a period of six days, the Israelis moved their army to occupy the Gaza Strip and parts of the Sinai. They also pushed back the border with Jordan and captured the Golan Heights from Syria.

IRAQI AGRESSION

In 1979, the Shah of Iran was deposed and replaced by Islamic fundamentalist Shiite Muslims led by the Ayatollah Khomeini. Tensions between Iran and Iraq finally resulted in Iraq invading the oil-rich Iranian territory of Khuzistan in 1980. Iraq feared the power of the new Iranian government set up by Ayatollah Khomeini. When the war ended in 1988, neither country had made any gains, but the cost to two nations was over a million dead with nearly two million injured.

Rivalries within the Arab world have often been caused by the region's oil deposits. In 1990, Iraq invaded Kuwait in order to improve its sea access. The UN Security Council passed several resolutions that demanded that Iraq immediately withdraw its troops. When Saddam Hussein refused to do this, a multinational force led by the Americans forced the Iraqis to withdraw. Kuwait City was liberated within the first five days and thousands of Iraqi soldiers were captured. Retreating Iraqi forces caused huge ecological damage because they set fire to most of Kuwait's oil wells.

Concerned that Iraq was developing chemical weapons of mass destruction, a US-led coalition invaded Iraq in 2003 and successfully destroyed Saddam Hussein's military regime.

▼ The US forces mounted a massive international military campaign to liberate their ally Kuwait when Iraq invaded in 1990. Preparation for the war was extensive but the actual fighting was fairly short-lived.

KEY DATES

1948	Independent state of Israel declared; fighting with Arab neighbours erupts
1956	Suez crisis
1964	Palestinian Liberation Organization (PLO) founded in Lebanon
1967	Six Day War between Israel and Egypt
1973	Yom Kippur War in Israel
1979	Shah of Iran deposed
1980	Iraq invades Iran
1988	Iran–Iraq war ends
1990	Iraq invades Kuwait
1991	Iraq forced out of Kuwait
2003	Saddam Hussein overthrown in Iraq

A SCIENTIFIC REVOLUTION 1950–present

The second half of the 20th century was a period of rapid development in science and technology. The age of the computer revolutionized people's lives.

Scientists and business people were able to develop discoveries made earlier in the century and put them to practical use. Business and industry realized that there were enormous financial benefits to be gained from working with universities and other academic institutions and important research was done through partnership between the two.

ELECTRONICS

One of the most breakthroughs invention was the silicon chip, a tiny component which could be cheaply mass-produced. It replaced old, bulky and fragile pieces of equipment, and enabled much smaller but more powerful electronic machines to be built. Microprocessors, complex circuits fitted onto a single chip, were widely used in electrical devices ranging from computers to space rockets and robots to telephones. The silicon chip influenced most people's lives in the late 20th century.

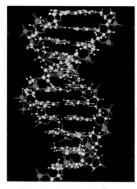

Since lasers were invented in the early 1960s, they have been used for a wide range of purposes that include eye surgery, construction work, mapping and weapons guidance systems.

▲ The double helix (two intertwined strands) of DNA was discovered by Francis Crick and James Watson in 1953. This structure carries the blueprint for life. The discovery is helping scientists understand the causes of many diseases.

▶ By 1990, many repetitive tasks, such as the assembly-line manufacture of cars, were being carried out by computer-controlled robots. This meant that industry operated more efficiently, but it also resulted in the reduction of the human workforce.

The silicon chip microprocessor was developed in the USA in 1971 and brought about a technological revolution. The chips were 'printed' with tiny electrical circuits that enabled computers to process and store information.

THE COMPUTER AGE

The developments in electronics also generated a revolution in communications. Photocopiers and fax machines meant that office workers could handle vast amounts of information more quickly than before. They could also communicate rapidly with other offices around the world. As electronic communications spread throughout the world, information became more freely available. By the end of the 20th century, anyone with a personal computer and a phone line could contact millions of other people around the world in an instant using the Internet.

In industry, electronics also brought about a new industrial revolution. By the 1990s, most aspects of the manufacturing process in a wide range of industries were computer controlled. Repetitive tasks on assembly lines were carried out by electronic machines known as robots. Stock control, distribution and administrative systems also came under the control of computer technology.

MEDICAL BREAKTHROUGHS

First developed in the 1960s, lasers were used in surgery to clear diseased tissue and carry out delicate eye operations.

In the 1950s, British and American scientists discovered the structure of DNA, the basic building blocks from which living cells are made. This led to the production by genetic engineering of new drugs which helped cure serious diseases. The discovery of DNA means that it will one day be possible to cure many genetic illnesses, passed down through families.

Genetic engineering also meant that new or improved strains of plants and animals, resistant to disease, could be created in laboratories. This technology is already helping to feed people in poorer countries. There are concerns, however, that genetically modified (GM) foods may affect human health. All GM foods must be thoroughly tested.

THE WORLD WIDE WEB

The World Wide Web (www) was invented in 1990 so that users could 'surf the net' quickly. By clicking on hot-spots on the screen with the mouse, the user jumps to pages of information consisting of words and pictures located on various computers around the world. Each of these has its own hot-spots which lead to further pages.

◀ The Hubble Space Telescope was launched into orbit by the US space shuttle *Discovery* in April 1990. It enabled scientists to produce images of objects billions of light years away in space.

▲ The first communication satellite was launched in 1960. The introduction, in 1964, of geosynchronous satellites, which remain over the same place on Earth, meant that any two places on Earth could be linked almost instantly.

▼ Search engines greatly speed up the process of finding Web pages and specific pieces of information on the Internet.

▼ People are able to view live video clips of a current US space mission from NASA.

▲ Many goods and services can be ordered and paid for over the Internet.

▶ Using email, people can send messages and pictures to one another across the world within minutes.

◀ Information on shows, films, zoos, circuses and many other forms of entertainment can be found on the Internet.

THE ENVIRONMENT 1950 – present

Unlike any other species on Earth, humans have the power to destroy the whole world. Only recently did people realize that the environment was threatened.

In the latter half of the 20th century, people began to realize that the Earth was in danger, threatened with pollution and over-exploitation as a result of ignorance and greed. At first only a few naturalists, such as Rachel Carson, dared to speak up. Her book *Silent Spring* caused a sensation when it was published in the 1950s. It showed how widespread the damage caused by pesticides was, and led to the banning of DDT in the USA in 1973, as well as in many other countries. Then pressure groups such as Friends of the Earth and Greenpeace also began to campaign. It slowly became clear that the environment had been seriously damaged.

The oceans in many parts of the world had been over-fished, and in many cases, scientists believed that for stocks to return to their previous levels, fishing would have to stop completely for between five and ten years. Car exhausts and factories pumped fumes into the air. Some of these gases mixed with clouds to form acid rain which kills plants. In many of the world's larger cities, like Los Angeles in California, the air quality was so polluted that a smog formed over them. Continual exposure to smog causes serious breathing problems and premature death.

On the night of March 24, 1989, the *Exxon Valdez*, a 300-metre long oil tanker, ran aground in Prince William Sound, Alaska. The ship leaked more than 35,000 tonnes of toxic petroleum over the next two days and was the biggest oil spill in American history, destroying wildlife and causing a major clean-up operation.

▼ Cities such as Sao Paulo in Brazil suffered from dangerous levels of air pollution from motor vehicles and industry.

Hundreds of oil-well fires were lit when retreating Iraqi troops left Kuwait in 1991 causing widespread pollution to the desert. It took a whole year to extinguish them all.

PROTECTING THE ENVIRONMENT

In the 1970s, British scientists working in Antarctica discovered that the ozone layer above them was becoming thinner. The ozone layer is vital to all life on Earth because it blocks much of the Sun's harmful ultraviolet radiation. It was soon learned that this protective barrier was being seriously damaged by the release of chemicals called CFCs, which were used in refrigeration and for aerosols. These chemicals have now been banned in the many countries.

By the 1980s, some governments passed laws to protect the environment, but some scientists believed that these attempts to protect our planet were too little and too late. Change was slow to take effect because at first people did not believe that the Earth was really in danger. New information was collected by scientists which proved that the threat was real. Clean (non-polluting) products started to appear but they proved expensive to buy and less profitable to produce.

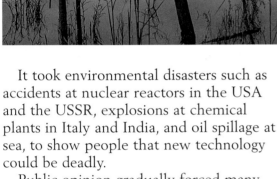

It took environmental disasters such as accidents at nuclear reactors in the USA and the USSR, explosions at chemical plants in Italy and India, and oil spillage at sea, to show people that new technology could be deadly.

Public opinion gradually forced many governments to take action and to reduce pollution. Laws were passed to protect the environment and encourage conservation and recycling.

▲ Huge tracts of the tropical rainforests in South America are being destroyed so that local farmers can graze cattle.

However, in poorer countries of the world, people's only income still comes from farming or forestry which often damages the land. Their governments do not like being told by the developed world to slow growth and reduce pollution.

▲ In 1900, the world's population was around one billion. By 2003, it had risen to 6.3 billion. In the year 2015, over 7 billion people will be living on the Earth.

RENEWABLE ENERGY

Most of the world's energy is produced by burning coal, oil or gas. These fuels are known as fossil fuels and there is a limited supply of them to be taken from the Earth. Many countries are developing renewable energy technologies, which use the energy from moving water, sunlight and wind. These are non-polluting sources that will not run out.

▼ Wind turbines are built on exposed sites where wind power is used to generate electricity.

▶ Solar power uses energy from sunlight to provide a clean, non-polluting source of energy.

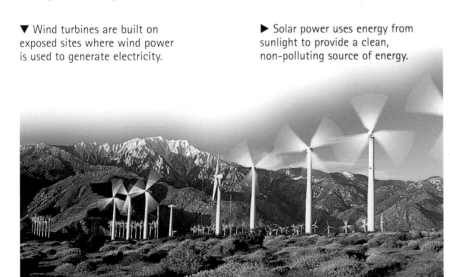

ASIAN ECONOMIES 1970–present

With the help of Western aid, monetary growth in the 'tiger' economies of southeast Asia was very rapid. It soon outstripped that of the Europe and the USA.

Manufacturing was the single most important economic activity in Japan. Japanese factories used the most advanced equipment and processes available, producing high-quality goods for export to the rest of the world.

In Japan, government and business had to rebuild their economy after their defeat in World War II. They followed a different approach to China and planned a complete industrial redevelopment of their country, and rapid capitalist growth. America had occupied the Japanese islands and encouraged them to move to a democracy. They also helped Japan financially and after the war the Americans provided money at the rate of more than ten million dollars a week. The Japanese brought in industrial and land reforms and greatly improved the education system for their children. Free elections were held and women were not only allowed to vote for the first time, but some were elected to the Japanese parliament. In the 1970s and 1980s, Japan's economic growth was one of the most rapid in the world.

Along with other stock markets around the world, the Tokyo Stock Market saw panic selling in October 1987. In one day, it traded over one billion shares.

OTHER ECONOMIES

Although it took longer to get started, by the late 1970s and 1980s, South Korea's industrialization was growing at nearly ten percent every year, far more than Western countries. Again, the USA supplied aid and Japan helped as well. Hong Kong also became a major southeast Asian financial trading centre, attracting a large quantity of outside investment.

Malaysia became a major exporter of both raw materials and metals such as tin, oil and natural gas, rubber, palm oil and timber, as well as manufactured goods such as electrical machinery and semiconductors.

Singapore soon became one of the countries with a high standard of living when, in the 1960s, it began to build up its industry. Shipping took a growing part in the economy along with the establishment of extensive oil refineries. Singapore became a major exporter of petroleum products, rubber and electrical goods.

By the beginning of the 1990s, these economies gradually suffered from the downturn in world markets. Japan's export-led economy, worth more than half the region's total, had been in poor shape since 1989, and over the next ten years, its stockmarket value fell by two-thirds. This inevitably had a knock-on effect on the other countries in the region and slowed their growth dramatically.

Built as a symbol of Malaysia's once-booming economy, the twin Petronas Towers in Kuala Lumpur are among the world's tallest office buildings at a height of 452 metres.

PEACEKEEPING 1950 – present

In 1945, the international community formed the United Nations to guarantee civil liberties and to work for peace and stability on a global scale.

Fifty countries formed the United Nations after the end of World War II. By 2005, the membership had increased to 191.

The United Nations was formed after World War II with the intention of trying to ensure that such a war could not happen again. It was established to maintain international peace and security, to develop friendly relations among nations, to achieve international co-operation in solving economic, social and cultural problems and to encourage respect for human rights and for fundamental freedoms. Delegates from 50 nations attended what was known as the United Nations Conference on International Organization in San Francisco in April 1945. The United Nations charter was approved in June, and the organization's headquarters were located in New York.

THE SECURITY COUNCIL

Keeping international peace is the job of the UN Security Council. The permanent members are China, France, Britain, the USA and Russia; there are ten other members who are elected for two-year terms.

During the 1990s, Britain used its significant naval presence to support UN peacekeeping and humanitarian missions in many parts of the world.

WORLD PEACEKEEPING

A United Nations peacekeeping force was used for the first time during the Korean War in 1950, and they remained there until 1953, when an armistice was signed. Further deployment occurred in Egypt during the Suez Crisis in 1956 when UN forces supervized the withdrawal of invading British, French and Israeli forces.

The first large-scale UN operation in Africa went into action in 1960. Belgium had granted independence to the Republic of the Congo, now known as Zaire, but civil unrest threatened the new country. UN troops were able to provide aid as well as security. In the following years, UN peacekeeping forces were involved in many troubled areas of the world including Cyprus, Lebanon, Somalia and Rwanda.

▲ The civil war in Lebanon between Christians and a Muslim-PLO alliance in 1975–76 caused much destruction and bloodshed. United Nations forces were sent in as a peacekeeping force.

▶ During conflicts in the former Yugoslavia in the 1990s, UN peacekeeping troops were fired upon by more than one side. Here, French UN troops keep a watchful eye out for snipers in Sarajevo's notorious sniper alley. The region of Kosovo has been governed by UN peacekeeping forces since 1999 and will be until its future has been decided.

WORLD TROUBLE SPOTS 1950–present

After World War II, border disputes and wars between countries continued. Sometimes the wars involved other nations who had strategic and commercial interests.

The end of World War II did not result in peace for all the peoples of the world. Border disputes and wars between countries continued. In Korea and Vietnam, wars involved other nations, such as America, the USSR and China. In other places, the superpowers supplied arms and finance to third parties without getting involved directly. In Afghanistan, the Russians moved their own army into the country in 1979 to fight the Islamic rebels, while the United States secretly provided training, arms and money to the rebel groups.

Many parts of the world have been troubled by civil wars. Families have been divided, economies have been weakened and torn apart by famine, disease and death. These conflicts have frequently occurred because political boundaries between nations sometimes did not fit in with traditional geographical, cultural, language or religious frontiers.

▲ The Tamil Tigers have fought for independence from Sri Lanka since the 1970s. In 2002, they agreed to a permanent ceasefire agreement.

▼ Indian soldiers inspect a captured Pakistani tank after border clashes over disputed territory in Kashmir during the Indo-Pakistan conflict of 1965.

In 1995, the UN sent a peacekeeping force to Rwanda after the death of President Habyarimana led to the Hutu people murdering around half a million Tutsi people.

CONFLICT OVER KASHMIR

When the Indian sub-continent gained its independence from the British empire in 1947, the division between Pakistan and India involved the movement of millions of people. Around three and a half million Hindus and Sikhs moved from their homes in what was about to become Pakistan. At the same time, around five million Muslims moved from India to Pakistan. Such a vast disruption in so many peoples' lives caused great problems, and the ownership of the territory of Kashmir, in between the two countries, soon came to be a matter of dispute. There were numerous border skirmishes after this partition, and India managed to take over about two-thirds of the state. The dispute became of great importance to the world when it was revealed in 1998 that both countries had nuclear weapons.

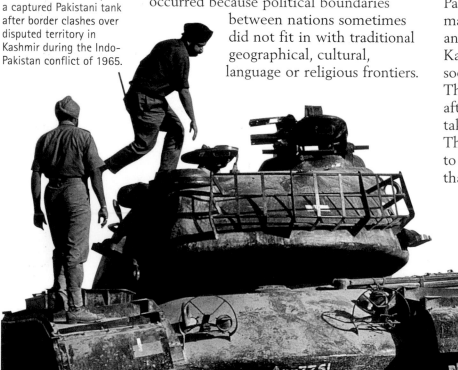

THE BREAK-UP OF YUGOSLAVIA

Following the death of President Tito in 1980, Yugoslavia was soon split apart by its many different ethnic and religious peoples all demanding independence. Macedonia, Croatia, Slovenia and Bosnia-Herzegovina declared their independence from Yugoslavia in 1991 and 1992. The Serbs declared war, and fighting in Croatia lasted seven months. In Bosnia, Muslims, Croats and Serbs fought each other. Thousands of Muslims were killed by the Serbs in so-called 'ethnic cleansing'. In 1999, NATO, the Western military alliance, used military force in an attempt to protect Albanians living in Kosovo.

THE FIGHT FOR FREEDOM

Groups like the Basques in Spain, the Shan peoples in Myanmar, formerly Burma, or the Eritreans in Ethiopia felt trapped within a larger state. In Northern Ireland, the Protestant majority wanted to remain part of the United Kingdom but a Catholic community wanted to unify the whole island. The 'troubles', as the situation became known, have resulted in the death of many people. The collapse of the USSR also meant that many peoples had to re-establish their national identity. At the start of the 21st century, many of the world's people still sought justice and freedom.

▲ Bosnia declared independence from Yugoslavia in 1992, against the wishes of the local Serb population. A bloody civil war broke out between the many different ethnic and religious groups in the country.

◀ Soviet forces entered Afghanistan in 1979 in support of the left-wing government. During the 1980s, Islamic Mujiahideen rebels, armed by the West, fought a guerrilla campaign that forced Russian troops to withdraw in 1989, and rebels overthrew the government.

▲ Although the war between North and South Korea ended in 1953, the border between the two countries is still heavily guarded.

◀ The Kurds are a tribal people of the mountainous regions of southwest Asia. Their struggle for independence has led to bitter conflicts. Kurdish refugees, fleeing persecution from Iraq's Saddam Hussein in 1991, were not allowed entry into eastern Turkey.

SOUTH AFRICA 1990 – present

South Africa was the last bastion of imperialist, white minority rule in Africa. The release of Nelson Mandela from prison in 1990 signalled the end of apartheid.

Frederick W. de Klerk (b.1936) became president of South Africa in 1989 after P. W. Botha resigned through ill health. De Klerk worked towards ending apartheid.

▲ Nelson Rolihlahla Mandela (b.1918) shared the Nobel Peace Prize with F. W. de Klerk in 1993 for their work in ending apartheid. Following free elections in 1994, he became the first black president of South Africa.

Apartheid, the separation of people according to their colour or race, was begun by the Boers in South Africa at the beginning of the 20th century. It separated the people of South Africa into whites, black Africans and 'coloureds', people of mixed race. Asians were later added as a fourth group. The African National Congress (ANC) was formed in 1912 to fight these repressive laws.

The South African, white-dominated, government brought in a series of harsh laws to try to suppress opposition. In 1960, it made all black political parties illegal after the violent anti-apartheid riots at Sharpeville. In the mid-1970s, the government relaxed its controls a little and started to allow some unions. In the mid-1980s, the government allowed coloureds into Parliament but not black people.

The ANC and other black political parties wanted a true democracy where everyone had a vote irrespective of their colour or race. P. W. Botha, president of South Africa from 1978, was the first white leader to want reform.

As the Archbishop of Cape Town and head of the Anglican church, Desmond Tutu (b.1931) won the Nobel Peace Prize in 1984 for his fight against apartheid.

THE REFORMER

Although Botha had brought in some changes to make life fairer for blacks these had not made a radical difference. His health failed him and he resigned in 1989. A reformer, F. W. de Klerk, then became president, and in 1990, ended the ban on black people's political parties, including the ANC. In order to show he really intended change, he also had many black political prisoners released from prison. One of these was Nelson Mandela, who had been in prison since 1964. De Klerk had regular meetings with him, both while he was in prison and after his release.

▶ Under apartheid, many black South Africans were moved out of cities and forced to live in slum conditions in shanty towns on the outskirts.

30

THE END OF APARTHEID

Nelson Mandela became the leader of the ANC. He campaigned for the civil rights of his people, but he also argued strongly for a peaceful settlement. By working closely with de Klerk, it was possible for both white and black people to work for change. In 1992, de Klerk organized a whites-only referendum that asked whether they would like to end apartheid. Two-thirds of the votes were in favour of ending apartheid.

After a great deal of negotiation, the first free election, in which black people could also vote, was held in South Africa in April 1994. The ANC won a decisive victory and Nelson Mandela became the first black president of South Africa when de Klerk handed over power to him in May. Although the ANC now formed a government, de Klerk stayed on as one of two vice-presidents.

Although a great victory for equality had been won, the new democracy still faced enormous problems, which would take many years to improve. By 2003, over 1.7 million children were still receiving no schooling at all, 8 million adults could not read or write, 6 million people had no constant access to clean drinking water, a quarter of the adult population was unemployed, and the great gap between the rich and the poor resulted in high levels of street crime.

▲ The modern city of Johannesburg is the financial centre of South Africa and lies in the area known as Witwatersrand, at the heart of the gold mining area.

▲ Supporters of Nelson Mandela celebrate the triumph of the ANC after the first free elections in South Africa in 1994. The ANC were clear winners and Nelson Mandela became president. He led the country until he retired, in 1999, and Thabo Mbeki was elected president.

◄ Following the end of apartheid, some South African white farmers were concerned that the huge farms that they lived on would be taken away from them by the government and given to black farmers in land redistribution.

INDEX